1-17

D0903566

Newts

Leo Statts

abdopublishing.com

Published by Abdo Zoom™, PO Box 398166, Minneapolis, Minnesota 55439. Copyright © 2017 by Abdo Consulting Group, Inc. International copyrights reserved in all countries. No part of this book may be reproduced in any form without written permission from the publisher. Abdo Zoom™ is a trademark and logo of Abdo Consulting Group, Inc.

Printed in the United States of America, North Mankato, Minnesota
062016
092016

Cover Photo: Brandon Alms/iStockphoto
Interior Photos: iStockphoto, 1, 13; Mark Kostich/iStockphoto, 5; Shane Cummins/iStockphoto, 6–7; Joseph Pulitano/iStockphoto, 8; Mike Lane/iStockphoto, 9; Przemyslaw Wasilewski/iStockphoto, 10–11; Red Line Editorial, 11, 20 (left), 20 (right), 21 (left), 21 (right); Alex Potemkin/iStockphoto, 12; Gary Meszaros/Science Source, 15; Rudmer Zwerver/Shutterstock Images, 16–17; Witold Ryka/iStockphoto, 18–19; Martin Pelanek/Shutterstock Images, 19

Editor: Brienna Rossiter
Series Designer: Madeline Berger
Art Direction: Dorothy Toth

Publisher's Cataloging-in-Publication Data
Names: Statts, Leo, author.
Title: Newts / by Leo Statts.
Description: Minneapolis, MN : Abdo Zoom, [2017] | Series: Swamp animals | Includes bibliographical references and index.
Identifiers: LCCN 2016941192 | ISBN 9781680792102 (lib. bdg.) | ISBN 9781680793789 (ebook) | ISBN 9781680794670 (Read-to-me ebook)
Subjects: LCSH: Newts--Juvenile literature.
Classification: DDC 597.8--dc23
LC record available at http://lccn.loc.gov/2016941192

Table of Contents

Newts

Newts look like lizards. But they are **amphibians**. They live both in water and on land.

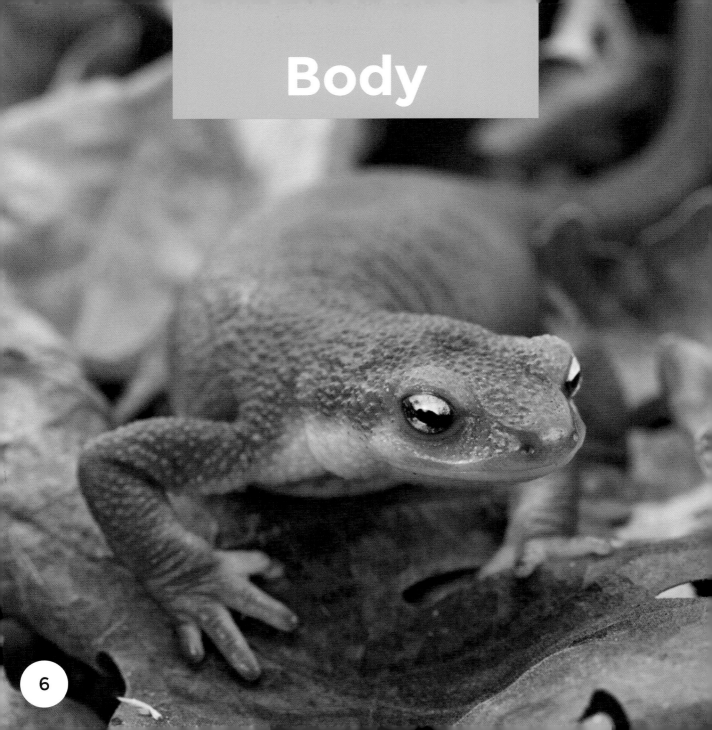

Body

Newts have dry skin. The skin is rough. It has poison. This protects them from **predators**.

Many newts are bright colors.
Some have spots.

Some have stripes. They all have long tails.

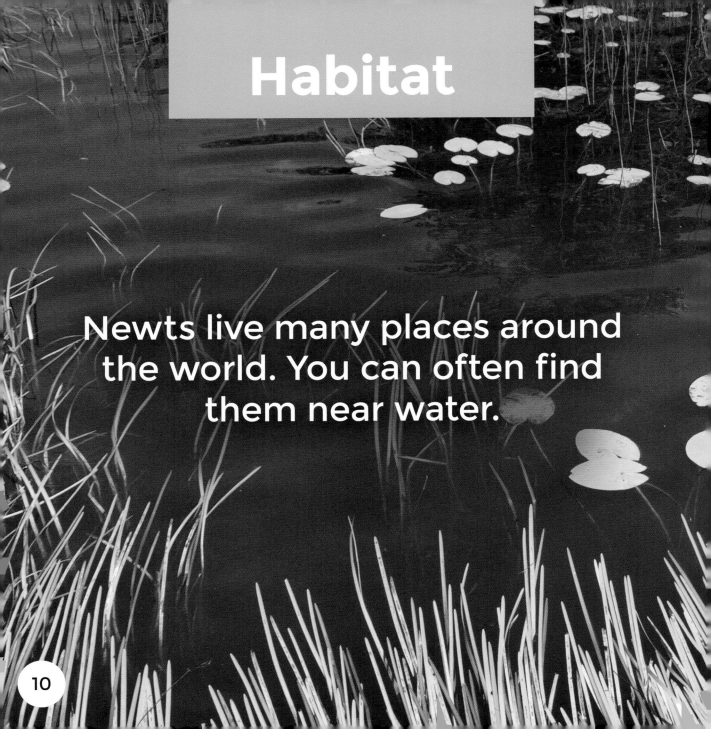

Habitat

Newts live many places around the world. You can often find them near water.

Where newts live

Newts live in cool, wet places.

Some hide under rocks or logs.

Food

Newts eat worms and slugs. They also eat snails. They bite their **prey** with sharp teeth.

Newts cannot move quickly to catch prey. Instead they hide and wait. Then they grab it.

Life Cycle

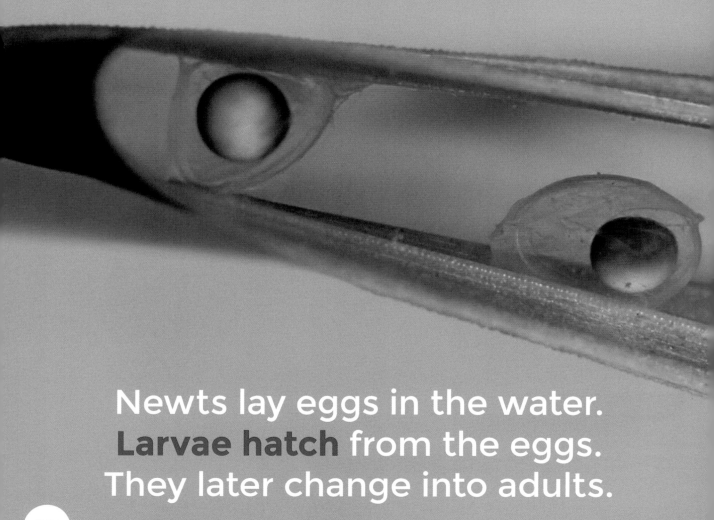

Newts lay eggs in the water.
Larvae hatch from the eggs.
They later change into adults.

Newts can live for 15 years.

19

Average Length

A newt is longer than
a baseball.

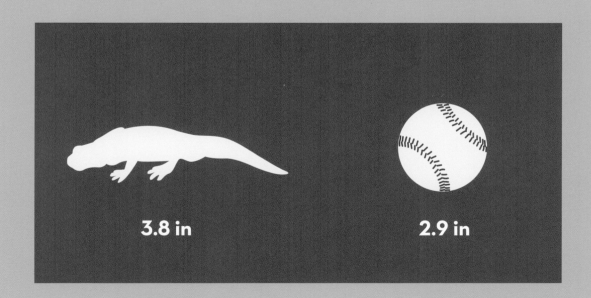

3.8 in

2.9 in

Average Weight

A newt is lighter than a deck of cards.

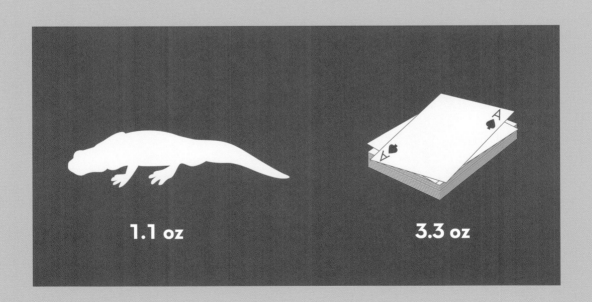

1.1 oz   3.3 oz

Glossary

amphibian - a cold-blooded animal that can live in water and on land.

hatch - to be born from an egg.

larvae - animals in a very young form.

predator - an animal that hunts others.

prey - an animal that is hunted and eaten by another animal.

Booklinks

For more information
on **newts**, please visit
booklinks.abdopublishing.com

Z**OO**m™ In on Animals!

Learn even more with the Abdo Zoom
Animals database. Check out
abdozoom.com for more information.

Index

24